lacemakers

Crab Orchard Series in Poetry
First Book Award

lacemakers

CLAIRE McQUERRY

Crab Orchard Review

&

Southern Illinois University Press

CARBONDALE AND EDWARDSVILLE

15 14 13 12   4 3 2 1

The Crab Orchard Series in Poetry is a joint publish-
ing venture of Southern Illinois University Press and
Crab Orchard Review. This series has been made
possible by the generous support of the Office of the
President of Southern Illinois University and the Of-
fice of the Vice Chancellor for Academic Affairs and
Provost at Southern Illinois University Carbondale.

Crab Orchard Series in Poetry Editor: Jon Tribble
First Book Award Judge for 2010: Jake Adam York

Library of Congress Cataloging-in-Publication Data
McQuerry, Claire, 1982–
Lacemakers / Claire McQuerry.
   p. cm. — (Crab Orchard series in poetry)
ISBN-13: 978-0-8093-3061-4 (PBK. : ALK. PAPER)
ISBN-10: 0-8093-3061-X (PBK. : ALK. PAPER)
ISBN-13: 978-0-8093-3062-1 (EBOOK)
ISBN-10: 0-8093-3062-8 (EBOOK)
I. Title.
PS3613.C5875L33 2012
813'.6—DC22
2011021080

For Jeremy Spohr

Contents

II.

Acknowledgments

Many thanks to the editors of the following publications, where these poems—sometimes in slightly different form or under a different title—appeared:

Mid-American Review ("Pearls")
St. Katherine Review ("Flying into Sacramento")
Crab Orchard Review ("Your Father Takes Me Gliding Above the Columbia River")
Louisville Review ("Guardian Home for the Elderly, Alzheimer"'s Wing")
American Literary Review ("Miles Away")
Comstock Review ("How I Devour You in Ten Minutes Flat")
Floating Bridge Review ("How I Devour You in Ten Minutes Flat")
Western Humanities Review ("The Train to Ventimiglia")
Harpur Palate ("Cassiopeia")
Superstition Review ("Other Women's Men," "What Remains," "St. Margaret's Well")
Damselfly Press ("The Bus from Strasbourg")
West Wind Review ("One summer we paint your house")
Relief ("Vespers at Brown Trout Lake")
A Face to Meet the Faces: An Anthology of Persona Poetry ("Blue Violinist")
A Generation Defining Itself: In Our Own Words ("The Bus from Strasbourg," "One summer we paint your house")

I am deeply grateful for the friends, mentors, and colleagues whose aid and encouragement have made this manuscript possible: Cynthia Hogue, John Nieves, Alberto Rios, Norman Dubie, Sally Ball, Tod Marshall, Daniel Butterworth, Scott Cairns, Aliki Barnstone, Gabe Fried, Daniel Tobin, Dinh Vong, Matthew Brennan, Melissa Range, Austin Segrest, Thomas Kane, and others too numerous to list. Special thanks to the Dorothy Sargent Rosenberg Memorial Fund for their generosity and to Jon Tribble and the staff at Southern Illinois University Press for their dedicated work and their faith in this collection.

Finally, thanks to my family—Maureen, Dennis, and Brennan—and to Gordy for their ceaseless love and support.

I.

Votive

The wicks are electric
in Iglesia San Dominic.

Sear of filament in glass:
tiny coal, a forty-watt

star. None of your cathedral
glitter, clutter of light

on the paving, this grid
of switches, little

circuit timed to twenty-nine
minutes and after, nothing

whiskered with soot. No remnant
but the afterburn, blue

on the dark globes
of your eyelids. Some

things in life are not meant
for such precision—the snug

dovetail of your joined hands;
the bent maple outside

my window, aflame
with leaf, its sheath

of frost; flickered
approximation of star—that dark

voice, and our reciprocal
lights. Trace elements

in smoke, fine blue
strands that rise, streak

the marbled mouth of a saint.

Cassiopeia

Once I carried the light

where I went   descending—

                  emeralds netting my hair—

            the staircase:

Chandelier.

* * *

I balanced each gaze

as weight   the way the acrobat

lifts buckets at the ends of his pole,

walks—   his rope suspended—

sky that spans the river.

If I glittered brighter for eyes

below me,

who could lay blame?

* * *

They thought I'd be lonely here,

exiled, arranged:

this empty ocean

from rib to wrist,

bone to bone.

I tell you

queen or constellation,

there is no difference.

* * *

Once my act was adding

gold by ounces—

circlets, pendants,

hammered thin and threaded for capes

and gowns—until my shoulders

ached with the gaudy weight of it.

* * *

All stories devise a villain.

Try as I might—

the sky dull and seething,

      the sea,

   tentacled

      thing

   (green as rot),

the rock,

   Andromeda.

Inescapable arc.

* * *

Love a daughter or love yourself—

    say what you will—

the same instinct.

My eyes, the white claws

of my teeth,

repeat in her.

Kingdoms after all

          depend

on queens.

Better that I survive.

* * *

Easy to believe a story—

menace

ash heart

ice mother or

    the wing-heeled boy

    part-god,

    my counter.

* * *

They thought I'd be lonely

here.

                              But I

size   to   sky,   cast

not   of   marble

but   star,   turn

above   Earth   perpetual,

each

bright   rivet   fastens

me.

Flying into Sacramento

In the final descent we're weightless.
Down the highway a line of cars
skims farmland, reflecting flooded rice fields:
each alone, then a double, alone.

Madame Babron, the high school French teacher,
watched from a terminal at Charles de Gaulle
as her husband's plane crash-landed.

Ecstatic fear is another weightlessness,
the knowing just before—the blip
and then its image.

Madame Babron carrying that moment
inside her: a small, glass bead.

At Christmas she taught us all the old carols,
with a despair that shook the notes.
One song returned years later:
a stranger's voice in a stopped gondola.
We dangled, the rooftops and streets
unclear and reduced below
like a postcard of a photograph.
Nobody moved—the song no doubt
taking each to a separate place,

as the song's echo does for me now.
From my airplane window, the fields
are darkly glazed: a kind of one-way
interview glass. How much of our lives
do we spend as watchers at such remove?
This morning over Nevada, when I looked out
to see a canyon stitching across the desert
and I counted the things it resembled:

a winter tree against the sky, the heart's
arterial netting, the deep lines in a palm that say nothing
of the future but a constant forking.

From Sleep

Tonight you wake to ocean
in the trees and startled,
without the usual defenses,
know that death will happen to you.

The way things turn strange in the dark:
your favorite chair a mound,
moonlight floats the carpets, your house

dismantled around you now, walls
peeled back like scales.
You do not cry out,

impermanence an extension of body.
In a tide pool once,
your father lifted the hermit crab

without a shell into your hands,
the unmasked question of its flesh
a thing you haven't asked in years.

The Bus from Strasbourg

Near dawn, the lines between things are softer:
     fence, trees, town no taller than a steeple.
You remember the newscaster's voice

while you dressed—*mass death averted,*
     chaos at Heathrow. The feeling of a trapdoor
knocked out beneath you.

Was it only last year you believed
     you could float, just a little,
if you knew how to ask the air?

The window glass on the bus,
     cool against your cheek, electric
towers rising from a cornfield like steel angels.

Every day the world grows more alien.
     Your body last week, in a room with curtains
for walls, the doctor saying,

We'll let you know. The body
     the one thing you imagined was safe.
You came from the hospital then,

windows brightening the street.
     The rush of men and women, shapes
you fell into, like looking up

when the sky has opened to snow.
     Outside Frankfurt, your bus slows.
Factories are smoldering castles:

smoke, brick, flame.

    As a child you dreamed of holes that opened
wherever you went—the park, gravel walk, front porch.

Holes as far as you could run.

    You would wake then, listen for a sound,
the whole fabric of things seamed.

To You, Next Door

I hear your water pipes early,
their occasional knocking
some comfort in that hour before light.

Weekends, the bump of a vacuum cleaner
against our wall—*our wall*, neighbor.
Sitting close to it, I imagine it evaporates—

our lives mirror floor plans.
Our identical gray doors,
the peepholes' one-way gaze.

Do you wander vague rooms,
feeling the urgency of wanting,
and not wanting, everything?

During an electrical storm, the sky
all violet ruptures, I lean against the balcony
wall, the one that divides us.

You're there. I hear your shoe
scrape something dry like dead leaves—
no doubt the same the heat sends off

the birches here at my own door.
Soon, I can't hear anything but rain
on the carports, wind's intense static

tearing the trees and I want to call someone,
hold my phone to the storm so we both
feel our smallness in it.

Years ago, my friend and I fell into the lawn
while gusts spun leaves in the Carolina
poplars and the trees' limbs heaved.

We owned every choice ahead
and its tributaries, all its riverbeds.
Neighbor, it was a childhood

ignorant of many things:
separations, compromise, even lightning
like the flare you must have seen

just now, there, beyond the power plant.
Or this one: an X-ray on lighted glass.
These matches, struck repeatedly without igniting.

Before Freeways

The light before she opens her eyes, the light after.
Muscles down his back like a magazine glossy,
carved marble in the sculpture garden.
She never knew him, sees that.
Outside the mower chokes on wet leaves.
She can hear its angry
mechanism: a grinder, an alarm.
This is only a drill, but still the panic.
Driving I-10 to the late shift:
are nights orange in other cities too?

Her patient, Betsy, as a young wife—
before freeways or swamp coolers, Betsy'd explained—
sleeping on the lawn all summer.
Dreamed she *was* Betsy.
Dreamed that glut of stars
casting a glow. Glut of opening
cotton pods. *Brutal. That heat.*

Tired of being the object of his—
tired. His arms around her
before work, a kind of owning.
Tell me you're helpless
and I'll let go. Struggles.
She can't remember
when he stopped using her name.

Every Wednesday the hospital
tries its sirens, emergency
lights like comets in the halls.
Her patient, Kay, waiting
on the collapsible chair.
The patients given compass points
and numbers. 3 West-17
who knew her husband better on paper.
4 East-9 who couldn't string a sentence.

Guardian Home for the Elderly, Alzheimer's Wing

for Karla

Lil pets the milk-eyed lapdog, believes
he is the child she lost at first snowfall,
1939, storm dragging in across the Great Lakes.
Most days she cradles one naked doll
in each arm. That ghost light in the corridor;
her open mouth, like the hole
a man, in rage, once punched in the plaster.

This photograph now in Marguerite's hands
(was it in her pocket a moment ago?),
a girl with carnations,
the brick walk of a model home.
Whose face and when? *It was,*
Molly recalls, *the rummage store on McClintock,*
how her mother fainted into a bin of furs:
the aunts fussing and clucking
and laughing too hard to breathe.

The women lay cards on the table,
no particular game, no memory of the meal
that wedges between their teeth.
Clarity, when it comes, is the voice that says
you are like that last piece of apple,
molared, always a little closer to the throat.
In another life, Rose says, *I taught piano.*

The Nurses murmur, cross the halls like sailboats.
Doris in 12B went quietly last night.

Today her children divide
valuables at her house in the suburbs,
dress each room up for sale.
A cactus blooms in the garden. The kitchen's
all white tile, and the four-poster arranged
like a bed from a catalog, pillows full
and smooth as if no one had ever slept there.

What Remains

When one season is at the brink
of spilling over, you recall
the way you walked,
ankle-high in yellow leaves,
a year ago, or maybe two—

it could have been two
months for all the lapse, except
the light, its bright tone
of between: the vibration
that gathers before winter's coma.
A kaleidoscope of Novembers—

where did you hear that time
is a thing like a crystal, the way
the facets are the same
when it fractures
into something smaller?

Confirmation class. A vine
and leaf pattern rimmed the altar,
the mantle green, for epiphany.

Here, Lichen and helicon moth, sun
caught in descent. *Teach us to number
our days*, the reverend had read—a hope
that something is saved
in the contemplation,

even if you wake
one morning to recall
the voice of wind in this burnt-out
gully, branches black, arterial,
leaves fallen deep
on the path over the ridge.

Traffic in Phoenix

Summer here is an overexposed photograph.
We retreat to interiors, listen to air
siphon through vents.
Like dollhouse dolls, what are we
but shapes taking up space?
I lift objects, hold them,
set them down.

From an airplane last week, I watched
the city grow large: circuit board. Onramps.
The freeway's glittering points.

Here the center is wherever you happen to be.
Every intersection a promise, fabulous
with lights: supermarket, gas station,
discount store. *When you don't need anything,*
Lena says, *you have to ask yourself what you want.*

I go outside, water my tomatoes. Heat and light.
Aperture, I think. Aperture flooded. Impossible,
in such intensity, to comprehend
dimension; the pupils recoil. Expressway
a swimming mirage.

I talk to my tomatoes to help them grow:
Listen. Traffic so constant
you mistake it for breath. Ocean eroding beach.
Where and how fast you'll be taken.

The Fast Local

Bone, found on a mountain, and behind her,
you: one dove, mostly feathers and air.
You know the silence; as an infant
it frightened you. Two wild

boys with the aisle as a headrest.
The mother behind us doesn't bother to calm
her glow in the glass, her snow coat
folded in a duffel. We lower our noise.

A girl is idle. The bystander
darkens the light inside.
Sitting in the wrecking yard at sunset,
the harp you see through the open gate.
There is something to her noise.

She tells you about the grandmother from America:
silk in hollows. Wilderness, an unfinished
ring of dandelion limbs
and this limbo of drab pastures,
partial, closed into ice. A telegram opening.

Feathers went whirling behind her
and her body to the last town.
Tea lights and cocktail
tents. She takes a car to the city.

Miles Away

for I.B.

We sat on the dock then, cider cans crushed
and glittering. As you spoke, your fingers
never stopped moving, lifting gravel, lifting
bits of glass into one palm. What did I know
about woundedness, how to carry it?

I wanted to split my ribs open,
on hinges, to pull you through.
Life is dismantled by moments.
The stadium in pieces on the river, blue, electric.
The story is breaking.

Dinah, your sister, liked sweet things,
let the blood and body
melt like a wedding cookie between her lips.
Now, the host won't swallow,
and sweet tastes only like her own tongue.

Your coat was cold when I leaned against it:
not resting and not embracing,
just two people touching, beside a river.
And why I think of this, years later
and miles away in a bar—

One couple gets up to dance. There's something
desperate in how they push
against each other's bodies, stepping
into one another and backwards
into the dark. All those years ago,

when you helped me to my feet,
face pale in the stadium's corona,
your voice carried its own rhythm:
I see that man again, he'll die.
Here. By these two hands.

A prism of streetlights, when we turned for the hotel.
We walked a little apart, each
globed in separate thoughts, and I remembered,
too late, the spent cans,
which currents, by then, were forcing out to sea.

Blue Violinist

Marc Chagall, 1946

We have come home from the cold, even children—
they float up the street in bluing
light, smoke from dinner fires.
All the chickens cooped and roosted.
The pigeon seller in his ramshackle rooms,
the baker's cottage with lantern
windows, a whiff of warm bread at the panes.

In my painting the sky is winter descending,
the clouds an open field for snow rills, a moon's
bald intrusion, fiddle's keen and glister over our roofs.
I stipple in a little heat: red
the hue of still-smoldering coals.

Whole villages abandoned, or swallowed
by surprise of flame, violent and complete.
First, airplane engine no louder
than the mosquito's whine.

After, stone wall, lone chimney, smoke.
I don't think of this every day.
Newspaper clippings, violin solo
unspooling from the wireless, or the earthy
fumes of woodstoves lifting on a cold morning
double me over in grief.

Somewhere under this sky I paint, I'm a child.
Father bathes first, and the water
glitters with mackerel scales
that swirl like galaxies or oil
sliding over the surface of soup.
His beard steams as he dries himself,
while I undress, shivering in my skin.

I lower into the basin and listen—
the rustle of cigarette papers, father
just through the curtain. He dusts
tobacco down the center of the paper,
curling each slip: a tube, little wider

than the wisher's bone. The oil lamp
casts a tent of light for his hands, as if
the raft of cigarettes, the knotty wood,
his articulate fingers, comprise the world.
Overhead, frozen bedsheets steam
and soften, uncontorting. Scent of lye and wind.

Your Father Takes Me Gliding above the Columbia River

As an engineless aircraft, the glider, or sailplane, is kept aloft by
naturally occurring currents of rising air.—Field Guide to Gliding

At three thousand feet the towline unlatches and we
plumb the sky, motorless: wind's pinwheels,
air's architecture—

updrafts that might lift us over the ridge. He's quiet
and kind. What fault sent your life in its stuttering,
a slipped nickel's elliptic?

In the garage, where we left you, you're sanding
the quarter-panel of a truck, its rupture
soon concealed under paint.

We lose altitude. *We'll have to circle back—*
all the wind's hoops in my ears. *It takes patience,*
like lighting a fire, one comes to it little by little.

Our shadow crosses cows, oily eye of their waiting
and drinking, men, stacked crates, fence gone
rust-wasted and rotten. Banking again for the ridge,

This column of air's sheared clean apart. We circle—as you and I
buffet the other's silences,
move apart. Some thick, invisible wedge.

There's wheat. Yes, at the ridgeline. *It lives on rain and daylight*
and requires almost nothing of the farmer—
more wind now than words.

Your quiet, your flint:
I want to ask him is it in the blood.
But the plane drones *no-no-no-no-no,* air whips

the cockpit's gaskets, we lift at once on some invisible arc.
There's the river with salmon
flow and speedboats, irrigation canal, glitter's

shrapnel across parked cars. I am already
thinking of the ground, not from dizziness or fear, but only
because I'm always thinking of the next best thing. The long

drive home, where light lodges its triangles and scissors
low in the boughs of apple trees.

Marriage Blessing

. . . if they succeed in loving the expanse between them, which gives them the possibility of always seeing each other as whole and before an immense sky.—Rilke

Your lips were painted. They
stretched to speak, and you rose
up from the ocean, a Chagall
lover, embraced, streaming
your wedding clothes
like a comet's tail. This morning
I couldn't recall the words, only
the vibrant green of the sky
where you floated and something
of that color in your voice.

You were married on a day
so hot the flowers drooped in their
bouquets. I was a continent away
and only heard the story
later, but as far as omens go,
I believe my dream
more than your hydrangeas.

Together, you seem whole,
the way strokes of paint
become *lovers*, a single object
separating sea from sky,
or perhaps drifting,
as Chagall wants them
in the scene with a large,
white chicken.

What My Mother Thought, but Never Said, about Her Honeymoon

Only the hands, palms
silver in the dark, are my own.
My body becomes a thing
on loan from another's life

just as these dunes,
snaking, always lapping
the shadow of the dune ahead,
from an airplane are mistaken for ocean.

I wanted clean music—
teaspoons against eggshells, an Alpine hotel,
the light transfiguring curtains, floorboards.
The desert, even its extravagance of stars,

a far cry from Switzerland:
cowbells are what you would notice
first—cowbells and snow. Tree flames
burning their way up hillsides to the ice line.

Reality: our Land Rover caught in the dust storm,
wheels spinning funnels in the grit,
our tongues like felt behind our teeth.
When we move to the apartment,

the freeway and its sounds
will remind me time is passing.
Around the corner,
the window of the theater museum:

A gown drips costume pearls. At the throat
a sea foam of lace the wrists repeat.
The best kiss I ever had
was years ago, just there, above the pulse.

Letter from Phoenix

Everywhere people are making love:
The upstairs neighbors whose bedsprings wake me.

The girl next door with the fat, Italian boyfriend
whose motorcycle does 90 in the desert.

The couple with an open window, late fall
when the days, perversely, keep warm.

I fish you up from the nothing of cyberspace,
unlocated place.

Smoke off distant brush fires and the dust
that rises some nights to gauze

the light from streetlamps
parody the fog we'd walk in.

East of the city, the desert's black teeth
break on the sky. Arroyos wanting.

I could get lost there, when no one knows
how far, which direction I've gone.

I'm running to meet you
in England, where rain makes its lace on us.

Your hand fits in my pocket—
exquisite object, those finely wrought bones.

You were married last August.
(An ocean at your back,

I imagine.)
Gardenia, Ophelia's white slippers. Someone

who won't, I'm certain, assert
herself against you.

See, I stand outside your life
without touching, the woman beyond a lit window.

Star cluster, highway, web.
We speak in metaphor until the metaphor

disappears. In the desert
light is a knife.

A horse's gallop becomes wings: flock of quail
thrumming out of the ocotillo's tangle.

When it rains, the creosote
is the sweetness of all things beyond reach.

Vespers at Brown Trout Lake

Across the lake a pickup
trails a thread of dust, curling
between two hills that cup
the dregs of sunlight like holy water.

Here, Eucharist threads
evening's weft, and cold
creeps off the water.
Shadows grow bolder, lengthen
almost to touch the priest's robes.

The only warmth in the world:
that one bright smudge and the truck.
I imagine the driver, a woman, reaching
for a soda can, one hand on the wheel,
acrylic nails tapping. The little girl beside her
wonders at the way her eyes and just
the tip of her nose reflect in the glass.

Nothing separates us but this
furrowed sky floating on water.
Communion. Body of Christ
dissolving on my tongue.
A glint and then
nothing.

Book of Hours

Christ, the pelican, bends to blood,
vermilion, finest strokes on lead
white. I turn from candlelight
to a whisker of moon at the casement.
The light fades early now in snow
that swirls and sifts the clerestory.

Around me, pigments, stoppered
and bottled—orpiment, ochre,
azarium, mussel shells of milled silver—
in the ring of my lit taper. Illuminate.

Dominus illuminatio mea. I fill the "D"
with ivy, helix, dipping goose quill
to dragon's blood. I'd like to believe
that these, my marks, will last,
beyond mildew and the gentle
feeding of silverfish. Last autumn
I found the body of a calf
in the river wash, flank torn clean,
her five ribs an exquisite,
white cage. Beautiful and dreadful.

Across the scriptorium, Thomas
snuffs his candle and rises in the sluggish cold.
Near me, at the edge of light,
a sheet of bleached vellum
awaits transfiguration, a prayer for lauds.
I will give it a kneeling Saint Michael
with silver spear and slain dragon.
For the spray work, calyx,
cusp, and sheaf. But tonight
my eyes grow dim, fingers stiff
with wintry indignity.

Outside—wind, the sea against the cliffs,
and through it all the bell for compline.
In the ring of shivering light things are
near and nearly transparent: my hands,
the vials of color, fish glue and ox gall.
The scraped calfskin
with blood-caked pegs.
I extinguish my candle and stand
to follow the bright stain of the bell
through the dark, carrying the dead calf—
that smell of its skin in the folds of my own.

Basilica

We don't see the nuns at vespers.

Their feet, soundless in the choir loft—only

the vaulted halls of their voices

cascading:

lustrous chandelier.

Desire has migrated, that is—

I can't say—

why won't you touch me

anymore? It grows: A pearl,

filling my throat.

Transparent church windows (saints and parables

lost to air raids)

through which the daylight enters as itself.

The walls, two old women, an alabaster

Mother of Sorrows can recall the sumptuous colors.

They are the only ones.

In the next pew, a man obsessively fingers

his thumb, a recent stump, still bandaged

and itching, I imagine, throbbing

where it isn't.

That our belonging, I to you, might be salvaged,

improbable as the two yellow dahlias

that bloom so late—

despite bare trees, lace of frost—at the garden's edge,

where a crabapple suspends

five chimes, the silver notes of their collisions

reaching me, sometimes, through sleep: *something's forgotten,*

something's been misplaced.

I wake and forget

even that.

Once, your kneecaps would fit

the crooks behind my knees as coins

float on closed eyelids.

Now, listen: a voice so clear

it aches, the way

an eye socket will,

lashes crusted with salt.

Stone labyrinth on the chapel floor

        and high overhead—faces chiseled in apertures

        visible to no one but the Great

        Audience, his hosts, and perhaps

an accidental sparrow, or two, that slipped

      through a sacristy door left ajar.

The open mouth behind that altar screen, holding one note's long arc

must be exquisite as a bone

splinter in a gilded box

or

the note is cleaner for being bodiless.

II.

St. Stephen's Hand

One coin makes
the locked case glow:
opulent, encrusted. Come closer.
Lean against the velvet barricade.
You'll see a cushion's edge,
the gilded wrist piece and know
the hand curls inside, shining
darkly as a leather boot.
The glass housing gives up only surface:
camera lens, faces of old women, revolving
fan blade. Turn away.
The relic's image in postcards, guidebooks,
clearer than the thing itself.

The Train to Ventimiglia

for Miriah

Windows float at the borders of towns,
bright TV screens that don't
see my seeing:

two play cards beneath a chandelier
whose glitter is
the sound of piano keys.

A man drinks alone—
his walls flicker with the golds,
the greens of yesterday's boxing match.

Mute, except, when the train waits to unload,
the Mediterranean's applause
on cliffs and beaches.

I have traveled since noon along this coast,
your letter in my lap. And in memory
again and again, the vacant house

when I came to find you, boards
straitjacketing the door.
My letters that return.

The isolate color
of a train whistle in the dark.
Has that saw died? The metal

teeth of your father's voice
across your sleep? I write.
You will not read it.

I write you the rowboats
that collide against a pier.
I can save you

no more than I could save
a lost child in the movie
I watched last night. I cried out

as if she could hear me
calling and turn back home.
At this hour, somewhere, you're asleep,

a scarf strangles the bedpost.
Your small hand uncurling
part way, like asking.

The Incorruptibles

*

Who would do that,
paint a pigeon and let it go?

The dance halls getting racier,
says Aunt Lil—same thing
the cab driver said
when you named your destination.

Lacemakers work overtime
so the Christmas markets
stay well stocked.

What kind of world is this,
where you can't find an open
pub on Christmas Eve or Easter?

Miserable wet, is what he said.
Everything's dripping, even the corner evangelist
in his stylized suit. He shouts for hours,
but later, on the tube,
you wouldn't know he's behind you.

*

Walking the dog, you ask philosophical questions;
gives you something to chew on. *I want*
something to chew on, I'll ask for gum.

Love how you make a point of saying
his name with all the vowels
accounted for: *Édouard.*

A*pe*-ricot you call the fruit—
I like the A softer, as in "apple."
It's your orchard.

*

When I was a child, we'd hear lions
roar across our orchard.
Father says they would shake the floorboards.
A kind of wonder.

My friend in Siena has seen the incorruptibles
enshrined. A reasonable person
might ask how they knew not to bury the bodies.
The answer is always don't quibble with miracles—

But the question remains:
who would paint a pigeon?
Better than a Japanese
fan when the wings go open.

*

Pigeon feed this morning
resting on a muff of ice—
plaza behind the convent.

The nuns make crumpets and tea
cookies folded as moons. They'll swing them
through the revolving hatch
so you never see a face, or even their hands.

They could be space creatures in there.

*God bless this meal, God bless
the hands that prepared it. Amen.*
This was Sunday school, this was
women with snack trays and crackers.
You wore your Easter dress with the pink
tiered skirts—a cake with legs—
but never joined the hunt, as some of the eggs
lay by tombstones. Somewhere below them, the dead.

*

The dance halls are far away
in a land with hospitals and soldiers, wars.

Did you know this château,
Chenonceau, was a hospital during the war?
The floor lay black tile, white tile over the river,
the beds all curtained under the long windows.

They say Uncle Lou malingered for weeks
until Aunt Lil came to raise him from bed
like Lazarus. When you asked
why Jesus wasn't a woman,
Lil couldn't hide her dismay.

Why don't you wear your tiara,
why don't you play in the yard?

*

Your well-meaning friends
taught you to pray: *spectacles, testicles,*
wallet, then watch.

Don't park your convertible
under billboards at night,
or you might find your car
filled with moths.

Birds won't molt in the cold.

Don't pick your teeth.
Don't sit on your hands.
Pinch the quarter between your knees.

*

When I heard the stories—
the chains and crosses, sacred hearts
flaming all along the mountain valleys,
oil drums set alight—until I saw it, unreal.

I can't describe how large those fires are
in the dark. *In those days,*
we did it to spite Mussolini, she tells me.

Your lady friend, the dancer,
sang an aria. Wasn't that your sister's name?
The one whose heart
stopped on the basketball court?

We don't care to tell that story.

*

Speeding down the autoroute
you come across a truck stop. The sun is out
so why not stop? Your opera ticket pocketed.

You could only afford the balcony—
the best seats if you want to know:
nearest the ceiling with swirls and chickens
and a goat by Chagall.

Who knew when we hired you
your French would be so beneficial?

Don't talk to strangers.
Don't cycle at night.
Pousse avec ton pain.

*

Bears and lions at the drive-through
zoo. I don't recall those car rides
or the lion's cries at night.
Chickens shivered in the cherry trees.

Keep clear of Italian forests,
vipers that spiral the branches—
their young airborne, undulant.

The Aurora Bridge is a magnet
for jumpers. The magazine
moved when employees complained—
their wide windows
opening to bridge and river.

As the papers had it:
Flock of Pelicans
Lands on Desert Freeway.
(Mirage they mistook for water).
That was the end, I assure you.

*

Death masks she keeps on a bookshelf,
another over the bed:
her parents' faces. Or the long
coat her father would wear,
now pinned like a moth to the wall.

Young lady, your hair is your nemesis.

As children we loved the *Britannica*
all the blue volumes, especially
B as in "body," plastic maps
we'd peel back in layers:

pulmonary, muscular, skeletal, digestive.
I've swallowed
pills bigger than that one before.
She keeps them in plastic compartments.
One after breakfast,
one before bed.

What did she say was the farthest star?

*

You've wondered as much,
coming in from the cold, your fingers
gone nerveless and blue.

Aunt Lil would make cider
and put you to bed. Cough syrup
stuck to the spoon,
spoon the color of pewter.

You imagined a castle.
You imagined a car.
You imagined your bed a raft.

The Other Sky
Mons, France

July.
Mothers lounge outdoors now because the heat—
their thighs enormous clusters of white hydrangea.
All there is: parking lot,
          the eaten skyline,
              scabby grass
                    they cross and recross.
Some miles away,
      the basilica cellar, an enclosure,

        (carvings even in the underpinnings), in which

fragments of antiquity lie

coolly, such marvels. Glass case where a woman's brown hair,

netted in leather and pieces of metal,

Merovingian, unburied with her bones.

    Waiting in her quiet hut

        or standing at the water, gathering berries, she would hunger

      for that other sky, the one that is not quite river, or rock

    and vanishes—

Windows' iteration:
a dwelling, a dwelling. *Habitation à loyer modéré.*
Urine in the park smells. A thing is just—
no metaphor, not even something as ugly
as *scab.*

The mothers are dejected, their daughters
with rings and skipping ropes
and hunger,

                                   closing.

Their daughters with faces of caged canaries.
No. Their daughters with
small shoulders.

One summer we paint your house

with the windows open,
so that tufts of cottonwood
sift into the kitchen with smells
from the Mouscron Yeast Plant
next door: not quite the scent of bread
baking, but all that warmth.

The man on my flight from home
said he was going into an oven,
meaning Baghdad. I want to tell you
that story but stop,
afraid he will seem comic—*Howard,*

Howie—dreaming an early retirement
somewhere off the coast of Mexico
(the long fish he would catch,
and the ocean like a bath)
telling me how construction

pays best in risky places,
the hotels he'll build for diplomats,
bankers, oil men. In that gray
light between continents he fell
asleep, little whisky bottles filling his tray.

Your kitchen is white: drop cloth
over the sink, tiles, odor of yeast.
It would be easy for us to accuse;
you would stop sanding the windowpane
long enough to say *vulture*
or something worse and wipe

your hands. I can't tell you the contrary:
that he was like a small animal,
caught in the teeth of a thing
it can't turn to see. I picture Howard
now, building hotels in an oven,
sand and burning: extravagant waste.

A van leaves the factory, bearing
those packets of leaven
to bakers, grocers. The easy
light on gardens and walks,
the gauzy tufts that catch it and shine,
an illusion that no one has less
than her full portion, that no one wants
more than his daily bread.

Waltz of the Flowers

It's been years, but I could
still sing you through. Older
now and tuned to the frank

reply gravity gives
every leap, no matter
how high—ready to be

merely one of many
onlookers, moved, yes, but
unremarkable. There

were times in childhood when
waiting for the older
girls in the wings, I'd hear

something of sorrow's small
darts in the music, how
the minor harmonies

let the waltz's grand swells
transcend, how the wilting
and release of spent

petals fringe Tchaikovsky's
score, the waltzing flowers'
bloom. The dancers, their thin

ankles flexing with the
spring of their frames, the lines
that make of their bodies

arabesque as swept as
calligraphy, humming
as a taut wishbone: brief.

Pearls

A storm shakes lemons from the tree, which she
backs over in the drive. She calls this art:
the smear of tangled pulp, the spray of seeds
like pearls. His own taste tends to pattern, charts.
To him she is like supermarket grapes,
their plump abundance, mirrored, tiered. *You are*
(she says to him) *that space of floor the drapes*
conceal: a stripe of light, the rug unmarked.
This is a beginning for an end. The stove
collecting dust and flour, slow rot beneath
the kitchen sink. The black-eyed Susans grow
too heavy to transplant, the spring's mild heat
more than she can bear. But most of all it's how
he hears *unlace* when what she said was *bough*.

Other Women's Men

Not that I am the type to move in.
Still, I can see why some women do,
brightening like the corner house that leaves
all their lights on: everyone knows

their kitchen walls are blue.
A flash of teeth or eyes that says
pay attention. All of us must hide
such hunger somewhere. Or,
if we are certain he loves her, the thrill

that he finds us interesting,
not for what we might offer in the end:
his question about my childhood trip to Russia
genuine, that hand he lifts to his glasses,
rubs around his neck, not affect but pure gesture.

I would like to believe this, as I crush the lime
over my glass, not trying to sparkle but not
not.
            This story about the car
he rebuilt in high school—

but people are all affect, I think
and then wait for sense
to catch up with his sound
so I can deliver the awaited response
with some extra show to compensate.

The way the young men at church,
newly married, avoid me or make
great show of wedding bands, why, at a potluck,
one whose wife is gone to her sister's in Tucson,
when I sit beside him, becomes deeply

fascinated by his pecan pie.
Some puritanical sensibility that sees an impure thought
far down the road and crosses to the opposite sidewalk—
even if that thought in the end is nothing
but a trick of sunlight.

There was a time, if we believe the stories,
when men and women didn't know their nakedness.

The afternoon in that shared kitchen
when I asked Sarah's husband about *Amarene*:
cherries soaked in syrup and brandy from the Friday market

and he crossed the room, holding the little clay jar,
unlidded it and lifted one cherry on a spoon,
the red syrup pooling the spoon's bowl,
and I opened my mouth to take
the bright fruit, closed my lips over the spoon,

only a moment, until a rat moved against a drain pipe
or I lifted a finger to wipe the syrup from my lip,
and we both saw how
close we stood, and he
turned quickly, setting

the jar aside, to scour at
the coffee staining
the sink.

Windshield Repair
Next Right

1.

TV in the next room,
a game show: *whir-*
clickity-click go the wheel's teeth
against the pointer.
The contestant's voice,

Go. Go. Go.

As if willing a child to run
from the man in the dark car,
as if her truck coasts on fumes
down the empty freeway.
She watches the dash light
and deepening snow.

2.

I think of you in the carwash
when there's nothing to see
but foam, the undersides of bubbles,
their tatted veil
slipping down the glass.

Look me in the face and say
you've never had a crisis.

3.

In dreams
my eyes, dry husks, fall
to be heeled to powder. Sometimes
you crush them in bed, rolling over.
Not the same as falling teeth,
to which Jung assigns a meaning.

4.

Open wing—
gift the neighbor's cat left,
garnishes the door mat.
Our door, their door, the ones
beyond, nothing transparent
but the peepholes.

5.

Look at me, I say.
The freeway going home, the freeway
I want to follow to its extreme conclusion.
Tucson, Tijuana,
wherever we find ourselves at daybreak.

Look me in the face.

Lightning and silence.
Lightning peeling the sky back to scaffolds.

6.

Another spin.
The woman with the wheel
pleads Go. Perhaps she's asking
a killer to put down the cleaver,
leave the room. Then a buzzer, applause,
her voice ecstatic, lifting:

Thank you for making my dreams
come true. You don't have to see
the fatuous glitter of Vanna's dress
to know.

7.

Don't let this offer pass you by.

It escapes us.

Wind in the office elevator shafts.
This TV priest every Tuesday at dinner
saying, *your life is a mess.*

8.

We wake to splitting light, lost cause,
blossoms of flame: the clock radio's invasion.

Most mornings I stay in bed
waiting for the empty kitchen,
your car leaving the drive.

9.

Turn it over in your hand,
the watch man with his silver
tools—clock noise cutting
the room to pieces—
opens Grandmother's Elgin
where the teeth interlock, all
its miniature gears.

10.

Pressure in your jaw like lodged
cement. You take it for a sign,
just as, months before the new millennium,
your father gathered rice
and sacks of rye flour
beneath the basement stairs:
the woman on late TV,
his insomnia, no accident.

Your father says, *there are no accidents.*
Your doctor:
you grind your teeth in your sleep.

11.

When we leave, smell of bleach and toast.
Cassette we bought the parakeet
loops our absent hours:
Hello. Pretty bird. Where've you been?

12.

I spend all day looking at interfaces.
At home I want empty walls,
walls like vellum.
Or the freeway at night—sometimes
I drive with nowhere to go.

13.

Turn it over in your hand, you say.
When I do, a gappy Brahms Lullaby,
notes breaking free like pulled teeth—
the music box loose on hinges,
its velvet lining come unstuck.

14.

I want to say: *Listen,*
I have nothing to confess.
Sometimes I feel like the woman
pressed beneath loads of stones
because she wouldn't.

I don't give it voice.
A *feeling is just a feeling,*
my grandmother would say.
If the weeds are clear,
peas need shelling.

15.

Look me in the eyes.

We vacation at the lake and pass
our afternoons without desire.

Ache of the wicker bench.
Cobwebs in the gladiolas
opaque as rice paper windows.
Porch swing knocking
where there is no door.

16.

Treadmills and stationary cycles,
everyone eyeing the soundless
screens, which beg us to buy,
which stimulate.

Friday, for instance:
the mother with boys and muddy hound.
Her kitchen sparkles—and further,
clean should be a bouquet
or meadow of blue
lupine, that sweet.

The detective pries a bloody
tooth from the sewer grate,
bags it as evidence.

17.

I keep a handful of worry women
beneath my pillow, painted dolls,
small—tooth sized—
made to carry trouble,
so you'll sleep.

18.

Our freeway routed over flooding,
swamp that was pasture,
cattle fence sucking into reeds,
then railroad, overpass,
tracks crossing tracks.

Your life is a mess.
A mess.

19.

Does your crisis recur
in cycles? Is it weightiest
when you're in bed, electric
fan in the air?

20.

Necklace of brake lights,
evening we climbed the South Hill—
a fair swath of air between us.
Miniature throughways,
the elevated bridge where trains crossed:
commuters, long haul trucks, tiny.
We might be the architects then,
a child connecting plastic tracks
for a racecourse or model city,
the toy cars he lets fall from his hand.

How I Devour You in Ten Minutes Flat

You leave me with the remains:
a half-eaten cake, its frosting
the smooth white of teeth.
Outside, a streetlamp comes on
and I watch your shadow's retreat,
the way it evaporates
into darkness. You've taken
all the vital things, refused the money
I folded into your hand for a cab.

At 4 a.m. you wake me with a call
from the station, your voice in static—
the last time I'll hear it
this side of the ocean.

Near dawn, I become a tidal wave
that falls on the kitchen:
plates in the sink, champagne flutes,
last the vinyl tiles. I mop myself into a corner,
then sit on the counter with a cigarette.

Nothing's left but grief's extravagance.
My fingers find the soft middle,
your name in blue icing.
I am a scoop, a fork,
a tongue. I am all mouth.
A swarm of locusts.
Nothing could be so clean.

Walking the dog, evening near the river,

the whisk of his retractable leash. This river's
smell is round, brown summer smell
I know from childhood and mother from hers—
long weeds and grasses that dry all day in the heat.

In the story a raven,
freed from the ark, flies for days
until its water-loaded wings turn back, collapse.
I don't name the fear that I am this bird,
bound to the place I began, and Mother
doesn't say she imagines the gray dove in my future,
that brings the olive branch once,
then settles on some distant continent.

She thinks of her mother—small, shrunken to the lines
of her frame, and that frame shrunken—
who will never leave her chair, or open the door
when she wants to go out, or dress herself.

Grandmother, exquisite in photographs, left
her fur coat, diamond shoe buckles,
gloves for hands much smaller than mine.
She brushed her teeth with baking soda three times a day,
teeth white as her pillowcases hung on the line.

Now the nurses put the toothbrush in her mouth
just once, before bed. There are other things they do for her,
and my grandmother, always so private, lets them.

(This is why my mother asks again
about that boy I used to date, the job
offer in Seattle, just across the mountains.)

The river beside us, steely and muted, has lost the light
and traffic of day, and I am neither glad, nor tired,
nor anxious, nor anything. Five pelicans rise,
single file from the surface of the water:
a strand of pearls lifted,
pearl by pearl, from a lacquered tray.

Saying Grace

In the car that morning,
before the heater began
its work, my breath
came in gauzy bursts.
Later, the basement of First
Baptist warmed to the radiator's
metallic complaint.

There must have been
song, a Jesus story.
I don't recall which father
or uncle stood up front,
only the way
he squinted at tiles on the ceiling
as if each were a window
to the congregation above.

The man with bow tie and button-down
pinstripes opened his mouth
and found no words.

And when they came
no prayer, just one
dimpled wafer, raised above
his head. *Imagine this wafer
is the world.*

He must have thought
the crumbs were world
without God to hold it
together. I only see the moment
between: a tightened fist, the way

the pieces fell to the floor.
The moment after, when twenty-eight
crunches filled the room,
delicious. This was
metaphor, this was chaos:
the storm of pale fragments
on vinyl parquet.

To My Great Aunt, Whose Funeral I Didn't Attend

To me, you were the aunt of appetite, consuming,
convertible open, the highway's giddy winds, or reclining

Monroe-like, flanked by men on some Los Angeles
beach, as you do in one brittle photograph, cracked.

Years later, our first meeting: your girth,
rocking down the motor home stairs,

your feet two cakes escaping their pans.
I can't picture their faces, the second cousins,

great uncles gathered now at your casket—only the hands,
orchids, cufflinks on some uncle's not-quite-black suit.

My family, nuclear, removed, never had "people."
Only your brother, Marvin, from Florida, who sends

postcards: *Played tennis today. Still puzzle our way
through crosswords. Doctor says it keeps us young.*

The last year, I'm told, your wasted body (carried nightly
to the upper room: your last denial of nature's limits),

was little but bones and fluids, body lost in its tented
nightgown. I imagine you like the porcelain-faced doll

you brought from your travels the second
and last time we met. Even then, veins

mapping your temples were rivers seen from the moon.
No one wondered that in old age you held, as your brother

does still, to a land of glitz and synthetics. *Vacation places,*
mother would say, *frivolous as high heels.* I imagine your tall

house, half-empty now on a lane named for orchards
long eaten by subdivision. Florida, my people who aren't

my people, what do I make of these but a little montage?
Winterlessness. Speedboats caught on bleached

film reels, the silver flashes of drivers against
a too-fertile green. Ponce de Leon's lost fountain.

When he didn't find that source of eternal
youth, did the explorer—an ocean from home—

console himself with a Florida orchid, the pearled
twists of its petals like the curl of a child's hair?

Or, sailing back to Cuba, poison from the wound
that would kill him leaking into his tissues,

did he roll over in bed, furious that somewhere
unseen in the peninsula's lush growth, a miracle

welled up, untouched, before sinking
back again into a hungry swamp?

Perennial Garden

Crocus

She turns the girl,
herself, wrong-side-up.
"Those were the lean years,
before the war, before
you were born." The back
is penned *May, 1938*, in square,
blue letters, a talisman
against forgetting (a petal
browns at the edges, fades
inward toward the stalk).

Phlox

In the photograph, she wears gloves,
lifts a cigarette to her
mouth. Sepia tones of pearl,
accordion pleats, buckle
shoes. Lilac behind her
in a city I've never seen.

Peony

She knew the litany of perennials
across a season. After mass,
kneeling in the garden, she
planted foxglove and delphinium,
her hands like roots in the newly turned earth.

Guara

She used to read to me in that white
rocker, near the corner:
brass stalk of the lamp, glass petals
cupping light, the cool gray
loops of my grandmother's Manhattan
vowels falling into my hair.

Aster

The year after Joe died,
I came to Sunday lunches,
watched the last half hour
of her garden ritual, the way the spade
seemed a part of her hand, the skin
across her knuckles glossed
and vaguely transparent, like tissue
paper wrong-side-out.

Chrysanthemum

What remains when the other parts
recede—a house at the edge
of a wood, the name of a daughter,
the work of our hands? Time
diffuse as light that gauzes
cobwebs at the window. Her palms
waking moonflower,
the skeletal coils of her fingers.

Room

for Lillian Doyle

When I try to remember you in whole,
I find instead the patient way
you'd loop a needle's eye, unspool a bobbin
until the thread's minutest click in its groove.

The same grace in every work to which
you'd put your hand:
pen stroke, carrot slice, smoothing of sheets.

Though I was young, I recall
the day your work room transformed:
pin cushions, brown tissue patterns,
measuring tapes replaced with paperweights and bills.

Your sewing machine covered and vanished.
With what careful grief did you relinquish
those things for good—so deliberately,
as was your habit?

You'd hold your knotted fingers to the light
in those days, as if
they no longer belonged to you.

When memory began to elude you too,
I knew you kept a note card for phone calls:
the questions you intended to ask in labored
letters, a line through what you'd said already.

You guided yourself in letting go, the way
a man I knew, when his wife was losing her sight,
would turn out the lights and walk her through the dark,
room by room, mapping their familiar paths—

I'll follow where you've gone
in time, know the gradual dismantling of self,
the losses final and absolute to this world.

I'll try to relinquish them with your
unbending joy, believing each loss
will be restored to me, just

the other side of this wall
to which, for now,
I only press my hand.

St. Margaret's Well

Binsey, Oxfordshire, 2004

When pilgrims arrive on bicycles, the lime
avenue is bare as an open palm, and clouds untwine
their wool, pale against a pale sky.

This man and woman, leaning
their bicycles beside the church, beside
the yew tree and St. Margaret's Well, the way
a thousand handprints darken stone, layer on layer:

the blind woman in 1265, who drew water
here and drank from the chalice of her own hands
until light poured in clearly through the trees; a miller
who once watered the cow that lived
to the age of sixty-four and never stopped
giving milk; all the lame and dying
who crouched or knelt

beside this same opening of earth. Rain begins now,
water on wood, on stone and bicycles.
The man pauses to watch droplets catch
in the faint grooves of a headstone
and wonders if miracles occur
only because we believe them into being.

Such an ordinary well, the woman says, and he
agrees. But there is something about belief's
persistence, even when myth has become
only myth. The water, in any case, is sweet.

They depart as they came, stitching down the avenue
in measured strokes, until from the churchyard
they appear in miniature against a sky
the color of bone, so small they could be sheep,
or stones in a field, mulberry trees to cut the wind.

Other Books in the Crab Orchard Series in Poetry

Muse
Susan Aizenberg

*Lizzie Borden in Love:
Poems in Women's
Voices*
Julianna Baggott

This Country of Mothers
Julianna Baggott

The Black Ocean
Brian Barker

The Sphere of Birds
Ciaran Berry

White Summer
Joelle Biele

Rookery
Traci Brimhall

*In Search of the Great
Dead*
Richard Cecil

*Twenty First Century
Blues*
Richard Cecil

Circle
Victoria Chang

Consolation Miracle
Chad Davidson

The Last Predicta
Chad Davidson

Furious Lullaby
Oliver de la Paz

Names above Houses
Oliver de la Paz

*The Star-Spangled
Banner*
Denise Duhamel

Smith Blue
Camille T. Dungy

Beautiful Trouble
Amy Fleury

Soluble Fish
Mary Jo Firth Gillett

Pelican Tracks
Elton Glaser

Winter Amnesties
Elton Glaser

Strange Land
Todd Hearon

Always Danger
David Hernandez

Heavenly Bodies
Cynthia Huntington

Red Clay Suite
Honorée Fanonne
Jeffers

Fabulae
Joy Katz

Cinema Muto
Jesse Lee Kercheval

Train to Agra
Vandana Khanna

If No Moon
Moira Linehan

For Dust Thou Art
Timothy Liu

Strange Valentine
A. Loudermilk

Dark Alphabet
Jennifer Maier

Oblivio Gate
Sean Nevin

*Holding Everything
Down*
William Notter

American Flamingo
Greg Pape

*Crossroads and Unholy
Water*
Marilene Phipps

Birthmark
Jon Pineda

Threshold
Jennifer Richter

*On the Cusp of a
Dangerous Year*
Lee Ann Roripaugh

Year of the Snake
Lee Ann Roripaugh

Misery Prefigured
J. Allyn Rosser

Roam
Susan B. A. Somers-
Willett

Persephone in America
Alison Townsend

Becoming Ebony
Patricia Jabbeh Wesley

*A Murmuration of
Starlings*
Jake Adam York

Persons Unknown
Jake Adam York